Going though love's motions…

Fredreka Jones

BookLeaf Publishing

Presentation by *BookLeaf Publishing*

Web: www.bookleafpub.com

E-mail: info@bookleafpub.com

ISBN: 9789358367638

First edition 2023

ACKNOWLEDGEMENT

To the people and person who supported me throughout this writing journey and pushed me to share and step out of my comfort zone. Thank you.

Write a poem

Write a poem. Sometimes it's simple, sometimes
it's complex.
Most times i don't know what to write next.
But then it hits me, randomly.
Like a nostalgic memory.
When she says write a poem
I think about all the other words I wrote.
Then Anxiety and ego are woken.
Stage fright becomes bright.
Especially when I think about the spotlight.
And the eyes are focused on me.
But then I think, if I never speak, how will they
ever know me, see me, believe there's something
other than me.
But I'm here.

I wrote that poem…

Where will this go…

2

Pondering, contemplating...
Waiting... hoping it still the same while I indulge
into my ways. There you go again Tryna sweep
me off my feet, instead I hold in concrete.
Stubborn to embrace, or just oblivious to this
game. Yet still I want to breathe your face and
clog up your space.
Till my unidentified love consumes this idea we
have in place.

Secrets

3

Secrets are forbidden.
That's why the truth stay hidden away.
Locked up, behind this protective safe.
paranoid to our decisions
Reckless with our intentions.
We start to give energy to the wrong attention.
Then the choices become undecided
Connection is divided and trust becomes tension.
All because the truth wasn't mentioned.

Subtle crush

This is just a poetic gesture.
Meant to penetrate the mind.
And go through intuitive measures.
Like the chills you get when someone give you
pleasure.
I'm not Trying to be extra.
Subtle speaking my words can tickle you like
feathers
Or hold you like forevers.
I only just met her.
And I'm thinking about the textures of this
energy.
And what it seems to be
She locks eyes with me.
body language speaks what our mouths can't
comprehend.
Out loud
Between these four walls and eight corners
It feels like my mind is cornered.
Is this vibe a pretend endeavor?
Either way I'm in for whatever.

Playing hard to get

The stares of your eyes, send chills down my
spine.
But what is enticing, you see.
Getting to know the inner thoughts of a confused
lover who wants to express in ways that are
different from others.
How conflicting is this when I can't understand
your tactics.
Which protects and distracts from the real
motive...
I visualize me being closer, indulged in your
circumference.
While your kisses imprint upon my stomach.
Suddenly I'm not so afraid because we're on the
same page again.
But only for the moment...
This passion is mutual, and this pleasure is
overwhelming.
Which is released on being free when it comes
to intertwining with me.
Your mind seems present in so many places that
are blind to another.
Yet you continue to use it with the confidence
you have left uncovered.

Where does your mind go, when this connection
meets?
Does it hide between your insecurities.
Does it wonder about the levels we could reach,
while your eyes rolls back and I slide in deep.
Take me where your mind goes, while the kisses
down each other's neck make our blood flow.
Only will the future tell such secrets of surprise.
Beautiful Chocolate kind, drive a person crazy,
with words that taste fascinating.
But only will this feeling deprived of what
supposed to be and reveal emotions that only we
can see...
I wonder if I really could understand thee.
Just thinking of this drives me crazy.
It's worth it, like a drug that can't be resisted.
To feel the silkiness of your touch and the lace
of your kisses.
Every glance we take as we pass, your stare
weakens me, weak in the feet.
Craving to feel what I've only daydreamed.
The theory is known that things don't come
simple.
Even though I know, it's hard to remember.
If we just be smart with this feeling, we want to
pursue.
We can resist the playful blame that we put on
cue: that it's all up to me, when it's all up to
you...

Tension in friends

She's a Slave to her attitude, that's why
everybody play it cool.
Her voice is a trumpet which blows my drum.
Conversation turns to plaster, which her voice
turns to disaster.
Now my mind is numb, how could I release
myself from the overdue past I've succumbed.
She talks, I listen.
I talk... no attention.
Now there's tension and everything I voice is a
lie, misunderstanding intervention.
How can I get through to you...
Or should I just look through you.
Like you do me...
I owe you something?
How could that be?
When I thought you were a friend to me.
But that's not enough...
Because you deserve to be happy and I deserve
to be stuck.
Your words wrap me like a rope.
Which you hold in your hands to choke my
hope.
Still I thought we were cool...
But yet I was just a fool for a friend.

Stage fright

the lights get brighter.
they say I should just get up here and speak my
mind
then my ego tests my pride
my voice begins to shake, and my confidence
runs and hide.
my self-esteem withers inside.
my shyness is hitting its all-time peak.
but I still speak.
it's like my voice is playing hide & seek.
and my legs start to shake & get fatigue.
but my feet still stand on the ground.
in front of this crowd.
I still stand here while my fear talks out loud.

Rent Free

Thinking of you,
The scent of your skin on the pillows
Lingering within the sheets
I think of you the most at night when the moon
reaches its peak.
and in the morning, when the sun begins to
creep.
sometimes i hear a car outside the window.
making it irresistible to peep
imagining you are about to walk through the
door.
although you're 1000 plus miles away from me
little things remind me of you.
even when I go to buy wine from the store or
when I hear your favorite song on queue.
or when I see the perfect view and all I can think
is about is calling and telling you.
so, when the day is bright & then the night slows
down time.
you kick your feet up living rent free in my
mind.

Infatuation

The way she impresses with her touch,
it's hard not to undress her under lust.
I kiss her neck, she grips my chest and say I play
too much.
her attraction arose from the bed, as my hands
spread across her legs
then she begins to beg as I make my way
towards the edge of the bed
Looking in my eyes, as her aggression fills with
surprise.
suddenly she replies " what's in your head"

Her perception

Please me with your eyes
The way her perception wraps me.
I'm allured by the way her focus traps me.
Now this tension is soaring.
Hold me within your views.
As you kiss me, I kiss you.
Each breath taken; I've mutely mistaken her talent.
The way she balances her eyes upon mines, I feel challenged.
She licks her lips, as her charm comes in.
Then she speaks her words, and the guard descends.
How could the way she perceives be so intriguing to me, how adoring...

Could I

Love is love but could I love you?
When you blind to the fact that
it hides you.
Defies the truth.
And make you cry too.
Feelings on the sleeve
Makes it easy to believe in you.
The attention makes me need you.
Although I should just want you.
But it's invested. I'm tested.
Pass the limit.
To see if my heart is really in it.
But I never stray.
Even when love fucks up the day.

Is this as good as it get…

tired of hugging these sheets.
let me hold you close to me.
locking eyes and clinching flesh
the way you stare has me wet.
is this as good as it gets?
Let me touch you with my fingertips.
the thought of me already inside
got me biting my lip.
gilding between your thighs
and fuck into a trip
intoxicate me with your High.
is this as good as it gets?
singing your name in your ear
calling you "daddy" is what you like to hear.
as you arch my back, and my climax is getting
near
continuously pushing away
you grip me back in your space.
and instantly I nut all over the place.
forbidden fruit is your favorite taste, yet.
the question is this as good as it gets?

Bittersweet

14

Salt and sugar don't mix
They just look similar

Sometimes too familiar
Hard to tell the difference without a taste
But all we care about is the looks anyways...

Bittersweet.

Connection

Tell me where the connection goes.
Does it Tingle in your toes?
Does it flow in between your legs where no one
goes?
When our eyes meet, can you feel time as it.
depletes
Warm hugs, and the charms into X's & O's
I can tell your body says yes and your mind
sometimes says no
But the feeling is so inviting.
It's so hard to keep up the fighting to resist.
The urge to kiss you then I miss you as you walk
away.
When will I see you again? My thoughts have
on repeat.
Lusting over you and we just friends
Meeting in these places in discretion
Does this connection give your heart that?
voided affection
Although our intentions, aren't mentioned.
We melt into each other's complexion.
wonder what's next as our blood flow thru the
heart in our chest.
You got me hot as I attempt to make you wet,

With simulating conversations, your Mind
indulges the patience.
Grasping you close, because I want you near
your shyness becomes vividly clear.
Your smile goes from ear to ear, and you laugh
with fear of this connection.
Although you've been rejected by those you
held close
Just know this impression is not a
misconception.

Hidden Pain

She screamed in silence.
Spilled her anger with ink.
Arguments with the paper
Constantly overthink.
She was tired, tired enough.
To say the words and spill tea

She failed to grasp the words.
Drowning in her anxieties
Trying to understand her scrambled thoughts.
Fighting with her insecurities

She was slowly losing herself.
On the way to find her own
Starting to run out of breath.
Finding no one around her
She was suffocating being alone.

They were too blind to see.
What demons she was fighting
Feeling as if no one could see her dying.
She was falling apart.
As she was hiding in her skin
With a Smile on her face, but sinking within

Dangerous love

It's dangerous to love you...
I go on and on in my head about these feelings,
only to feel myself drown.
the feeling when your presence is around fills a
void.
To the top, so full, it's irresistible to stop.
Infatuated with your intellect, beginning to catch
myself staring.
I become oblivious to your looks and the skin
you're wearing.
 Your eyes gleaming when you hold me.
But love still leaves me lonely.
So it's dangerous to love you. …
You're like a drug, and I'm the addict.
Stuck, love holds me in chains.
Ready to pull my wrist when I try to get away.
This begins to become a habit.
Refusing to go to rehab.
I start to lose my sane
Like I just got to have it, have you?
This feeling is melting my brain.
But "you'll hold me together" she say.
Till she kidnaps my heart and run away.
Now I'm fragile.
and I'm still thinking it's dangerous to love you.

Untitled

19

Open up, open wide,
can you think with an open mind?
 Closed up, closer.
can I talk to you close up...

I'm free but I'm scared

I'm free from you, and scared.

I'm still in love, can't you tell?
Friends deceive, relationships fail.
Off balance, so I fell.
One peak, tripped over the rail.
No hammer, landed on a nail.
No weight zeroed out the scale.
No stamps, return to sender mail.
No stamps delayed every meal.
No touch, like you were a male.

Conversations, distant in the air
Met a new one, with some pretty hair.
Her body, damn! Yes, I mean to stare.
Ignore her logics, like I didn't care.
Ignore my watches, got no time to spare.
Became so naughty, like she under spell
tell her I'm stuck; life is not fair.
Stuck on you, headed to despair.
Cherished every move, that's pretty rare
My heart locked, no argument there.

I'm feeling that shit strong like this drink.

Love overcoming my thoughts, I have to remind
myself to think
Remind myself to blink.
To eat
Then repeat.
Shit I forgot to breath.
Man, just hurry and fucking leave!

She thinks I'm overreacting with the breathing.
I think she under reacts when She see me
leaving.
So busy learning these bitches, plotting and
linking.
Just know that you're a part of this constant
overthinking.

But don't come looking for me when I say I am
done.
I love you then I hate you for only two reasons.
For loving me then hurting me right where I
begun
"I'm free from you, and scared." Guess where I
got that from

I know you love me, but that's just what I felt.
Looking into your eyes makes me fucking melt.

You touch me, here comes those feelings I try to
amend.

You kiss me, now I'm drifting off into the deep
end.
You love me, now I'm falling for you once
more. Third time... AGAIN!

The past

The Past...
Memories of you lingering in my mind
Makes me wonder if I miss you...
I shouldn't but you don't know that.
You have your thoughts and I know you do. You
afraid to tell me, I'm afraid to tell you.
But I love you, so Ima plays it cool.
While you act like you don't know me, know
you...
But I feel it. I do
You were the light that shined so bright in my
soul...
But that light has dimmed, and I
guess I got to let you go.
As now we are strangers and lovers no more.
A piece of my heart you'll be, even though you
feel this hate for me.
I feel you as the beautiful flower you bloomed
out to be...
To you, sincerely......

Healing…

I am slowly learning how to be alone.
I am slowly learning how to wake up in the
middle of the bed.
How to make just be one with the mornings.
How to hold my own heart, how to take up my
own space.
I am slowly learning how to stop filling voids
with other human beings, and instead, I am
slowly learning how to confront the void itself.
How to heal it.
I am slowly learning what it means to be human.
What it means to make mistakes and learn from
them.
What it means to be both happy and sad at the
same time.
I am slowly learning how to do the work,
instead of soaking in the hurt.
How to stop running from what is heavy and
uncomfortable in my life.
How to take the easy route less and less.
How to stay out of the comfort zone
How to fix my own mess.
How to grow myself, how to be a better person.

9 789358 367638